Oscar's 40 Poems

By Oscar Channer

To
My family

Table of Poems

THE HUMAN PIG

COWS

MR. MILLY MILLER

MINING

TRACES

THE NIGHT

TROUBLE

DIRTY GARAGE

GROSS LIVING ROOM

SCRIBBLE

PICKING HOX

SIT IN A PIT

HEADS OR TAILS

FIFTY FEET TALL

DRAG BACK

SPACE

FAKE COIN MAKER BEN

The Mean Hen

She would try to eat
Every single trout
When she did not get
Her way she would pout.

She was also very
Unhappy and mean
She was neither
Neat or clean

She would lay atomic
Eggs that went "BAM"
She also picked on
Pour little Sam.

Babies

Why do they pull your hair?
Why do they take your underwear?

They take naps
They sob and cry
When they're older
They like to lie.

Messy Bedroom

There is an
Unmade bed.
A gum wrapper
Some string and lead.

Some stinky socks
A purple string
A rotten apple and
Some random thing

A smelly dresser
A stick of gum
My rocking horse
And rotten chum

Nails and pails
Fifty clocks
Some silverware
And Dads old socks.

Some pencils
Some quills
A peace of paper

I found some pills!

A couple twigs
A broken cup
A baseball bat
And a toy pup

Now I know
A place of doom
It is my brothers
Bedroom!

The Worst Place Ever

It gives me a
Big spine shiver
It also kind of
Gives me a quiver

It smells like
Sixty rats in a stew
And three year
Old doggy's doo!

You might get
Some funky static
In the worst place
Called the attic!

Little Brothers

They terrorize you
They will not go away
They copy you
They will soon pay.

The Day

Get out of bed
It's the day
Its fun and
I like to play!

England

The awesome land
With castles
England is grand!

Guards and knights
Rainy a lot
Chocolate bites.

Rugby Football
Tennis and Squash
They have a mall.

Was Them Not Me

When somebody says you did a good
deed.
When it was somebody not you I
guaranteed.
Do not try to get her back.
Or you are cutting some slack.

I will give you advice it will cool you down
with rice.
So you are guaranteed to do a good
deed and not get your love.
Who is as sweet as a dove!
So try your best indeed!

Stinky Shower

What is that smell
Is it old men's gel?

Is it rats is it goo
Hope its not doggy poo!

Is it a garbage heap?
It sounds like it made a beep.

I went upstairs looked inside
"Yuck!" disgusting I saw a mud pie.

Science

What is Science?
Science is biology.
You do experiments.
Science is geology.
Magnets and space!
It is all science.
Even your face!

The Night Fight

If you fight
In the night
And you have no light
It can be such a fright!

The Silly Pants

The Silly Pants
Could somewhat walk
The silly pants
Could also talk.

The Silly Pants
Liked Mr. Shorts
The silly pants
Liked all sorts.

Then when Silly
Pants got ants
He was not silly pants'
He was angry pants'.

He would blow
A fuse. Make
A fuss. Oh for
Heaven sake…

He was Silly Pants.

Seasons

Birds start to sing in the awesome spring.
In the winter watch out don't get a
splinter!
In the fall bee careful playing on the wall!
There's no bummer about summer!
And those are all the seasons of the year.

The Famous Zoo

Mr. Dippy Diddly Doo
Had the most famous zoo.

The floors all shine
They sell free whine.

A list of animals: The Cataroos,
The Speedy Snail and the Corkadoos.

There are a way lot more
But I don't want to make you snore.

Now you know the famous zoo
Of Mr. Dippy Diddly Doo!

The Human Pig

In the mud
Or the Gutter
I shove my face
With butter!

An apple core
Is very yum!
I am a human pig
So I ate ABC gum!

He got a huge
Big stomachache
That caused a
Big earthquake!

And he died!

Cows

Cows go moo.
And they sometimes have to go poo.
Wear boots near their habitat.
Or you will regret that.
They eat grass.
They have a mass of grass to eat.
Cows go moo.
And look out for there poo!
You got to bless.
Not to step in there messy mess.
Cows give you milk.
But not silk.
And I love cows!

Mr. Milly Miller

Mr. Milly Miller
Married a caterpillar.
A million people came to the wedding.
The caterpillar fixed the bedding.
When Mr. Milly Miller had a long day at
work
He went totally berserk.
The caterpillar loved to bake
Mr. Milly Miller stuffs his face with cake.
I will give you advice
Never meet him he's not nice.
That's the story of Mr. Milly Miller
Who married a caterpillar!

Mining

All those caves'
Filled with fun.
All those crystals
Theirs a ton!

Theirs rubies and gems
Silver and gold
Shining objects
There might be some mold.

Static mites and static tits
Our part of a cave
If you find a crystal
Do me a fav…

Give it to me!

Traces

One trace,
Two traces.
Oh no!
My shoelace.
Three traces
Look at my
Masterpiece!

The Night

My mom walked out
Turned off the light
I was scared because
It was the night!

I ran to the door
But it was locked
I tried hard to get
Out I even knocked.

I tried to go to bed.
It was hard when I
Was not fed.

I just lay there
Sadly in the dark
I started to dream
I was at the park.

I fell asleep
And did not make a peep.

Trouble

If you lie
Hit or punch
Make a sound
That goes crunch
If you're bully
Or a sore winner
Or you just
Ruined dinner.
If you're mean
If you're rude
You're a really
Bad dude.
Now you know
What is trouble!
Don't pop your
Moms bubble!

Dirty Garage

A van a car
Some sticky tar
A broken back door
A stinky floor
Seven filthy flies
Sixteen perfect pies
A big gas tank
A weird piggy bank
A pink balloon
A little spoon
A huge ball
That's three feet tall
A bell that rang
I heard a bang
A makeup kit
A candle that's lit
A water leak
A huge red streak
A kickstand
A broken band

Some smelly clocks

A dresser of socks
A big gold medal
A small bike pedal
A heed stop sign
It was a little shrine
This garage indeed
My brothers guaranteed.

Gross living room

Purple pail
A greasy chair
Toenails and
Long hair.

Polished plants
Ladies shoes
And also
The news.

I think
This living room
Needs to be
Vacuumed!

Scribble

Right left
Warp weft.
Everywhere
Even there
Zing zang
Bing bang
Scribble.

Picking Hox

Itch and itch
Pick and pick
Somebody give me
A scratching stick!

It's not anything
Like chicken pox
It's called
Picking Hox

It hurts it
Burns it kills
Somebody give
Me pills!

Don't touch me
If you do I'll say ow
Then after that
I will say yow.

I hope they
Find a cure

Because today
I have a tour!

Sit in a Pit

If you sit
In a pit
And you spit
You'll get a zit
You'll get bit
If you sit
In a pit!

Heads or Tails

If you flip Heads
You'll get two beds
If you flip Tails
You'll be squashed bye whales.

Fifty Feet Tall

You don't want to
Be fifty feet tall
Because then everyone
Will look super small.
You would have the
Most horrible gas
It would take up an
Acre of mass
So that's why you don't
Want to be fifty feet tall.

Drag back

Roll the ball
Back "Retreat!"
Kick the ball
Away from your feet!

Space

Dwarf planets
And the sun
Hope Pluto doesn't
Taste like a hotdog bun.

Bright stars
Exploding Io
This poem is
Not a bio.

Lonely Eris
Happy Earth
Without the moon
You wouldn't surf!

Fake Coin Maker Ben

He'd make coins look
Real when it was fake!
That's his job so
That's what he'd make.

Devil

Look out
There's the Devil!
Get in your cars
And push down on
The pedal.
He will take
You down
To the
Under ground
So drive away!
From the devil!

Falcon

Falcon was in
A very bad mood!
Maybe it was be-
Cause he had no food.
Falcon made a
Fuss and a riot
Everyone thought
He was on a diet.
Then Falcon sat
Down and cried.
Because he thought
He had just died.

The Pilot

Are pilot's name was Bob
And he was a big old slob.
He did not know how to count
He did not knowhow to amount.
He did not learn his math.
I think Bob is very daft.
That's a story of are pilot
Who was a very big riot!

Tickle Time

He tickled me so
I tickled him.
Then my mom
Tickled Mr. Jim.
Then Mr. Jim
Tickled Derek
Then Derek
Tickled Eric.
Then Eric went by
And tickled Mary
Then Mary tickled
Crazy Mary.
That whole day
Was a rhyme
And it's called
Tickle Time.

Skiing

If you go skiing
You will be yipping
Skiing is very fun
You don't want to be done.
So if you go skiing
Try to be yipping.

The Ski Dip

I went skiing and
There was a dip
I hope I don't
Break a hip!

Roller Coasters

Steep quick turns
You lose your belly
Sometimes you
Feel like jelly!
Loop de loop
Take a drop
Will this coaster
Ever stop?
Now it stopped,
I feel dizzy
All my blood is
Getting fizzy!

Socks

Put them on
Rub and get static
They get nice and
Cozy Automatic
Take them off
Your feet feel old
Your socks were hot
But now your feet are cold.

My Dad Says Some Strange Words

My dad says some
Strange little words
Sometimes names
Of birds!
Ski house, Television,
Cobalt, Snore,
Pompeii, Platinum
And stuff galore!

Sorry but it is…

THE END